D0953416

.50

AFRICAN GREY PARROTS
KW-018

CONTENTS

Photo Credits: Covers by Horst Mueller. Inside front end papers by San Diego Zoo. Back end papers by C.L.I. Frontispiece by Harry Lacey.

ISBN 0-87666-977-1

KW-018

© 1979 by T.F.H. Publications, Inc. Ltd.

Distributed in the U.S. by T.F.H. Publications, Inc., 211 West Sylvania Avenue, P.O. Box 427, Neptune, N.J. 07753; in England by T.F.H. (Gt. Britain) Ltd., 13 Nutley Lane, Reigate, Surrey; in Canada to the book store and library trade by Beaverbooks, 953 Dillingham Road, Pickering, Ontario L1W 1Z7; in Canada to the pet trade by Rolf C. Hagen Ltd., 3225 Sartelon Street, Montreal 382, Quebec; in Southeast Asia by Y.W. Ong, 9 Lorong 36 Geylang, Singapore 14; in Australia and the South Pacific by Pet Imports Pty. Ltd., P.O. Box 149, Brookvale 2100, N.S.W., Australia; in South Africa by Valiant Publishers (Pty.) Ltd., P.O. Box 78236, Sandton City, 2146, South Africa; Published by T.F.H. Publications, Inc., Ltd., The British Crown Colony of Hong Kong.

African
GREY PARROTS

PAUL R. PARADISE

(1) Famous bird trainer Risa Teitler holding an Amazon and African Grey. Photo by Dr. Herbert R. Axelrod. (2) Typical African Grey. Photo by Harry Lacey. (3) African Grey showing grasping ability of its foot and its utilization of the four toes (two in front and two around back of piece of banana). Photo by Horst Mueller.

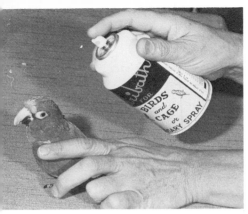

African Greys are probably the best of all talking parrots, and they make excellent pets. But keeping a parrot is not all fun. They must be kept clean to help prevent infestation by parasites. Above another type of parrot (Halfmoon Conure) is being sprayed with an anti-pest aerosol spray.

Introduction

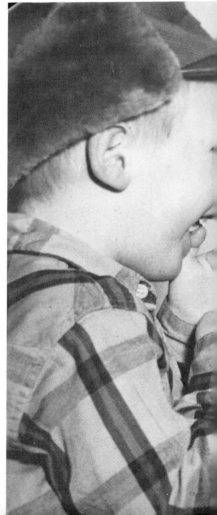

The Talking Bird

The African Grey Parrot *(Psittacus erithacus erithacus)*, which has the reputation of being the best of the talking parrots, has been a popular cage bird for a long time, especially in Europe. Until recently, because of regulations on bird importation, the popularity of the African Grey in the United States was eclipsed by that of the more colorful parrots of South America, particularly birds of the genus

STEPS IN TRAINING YOUR AFRICAN GREY PARROT. (1) Get the bird's attention. If he persists in ignoring you (2) gently grasp his beak and force him to pay attention. All the while you should be repeating over and over the same phrase that you want to teach him (3 and 4). Keep repeating the same phrase while you handle him.

To teach your African Grey to handle easily, you should have it perch on your two clasped hands, with one foot on each hand (5), then slowly separate your hands (6) and (7) so the bird is forced to climb onto one hand. If you hold your hands too far apart (8) the bird will be inclined to use its bill to assist in climbing.

Amazona, better known as Amazons. Three birds in particular, both members of the genus *Amazona,* are very popular cage birds in the United States: the Panama parrot *(Amazona ochrocephala panamensis),* the yellow-naped Amazon parrot *(A. o. auropalliata)* and the Mexican double yellow head *(Amazona o.oratrix).* These birds are great talkers, as are the other Amazons.

Although the Amazons are more colorful, the African Grey's reputation lies in its talking ability. The *Guiness Book of World Records* recently gave undisputed claim of world champion talker to an African Grey named "Prudle" who had a thousand-word vocabulary.

The African Grey's voice is not "nasal" like the speaking voice of the Amazons. Additionally, the Grey's voice possesses a wide range of possible sounds. Some experts have even compared its tonality to that of the human voice.

Greys have the remarkable capacity to learn sounds on their own. There are many recorded instances of the Grey imitating a dog or an owl, for instance, with such clarity that even the bird's owners were fooled. Bob Novak, of Novak's Aviaries, Long Island, is an importer of African Greys. He keeps many as pets and reports that his birds' talking has fooled his own children many times. They will be outside playing and, hearing their mother calling for them, will run inside only to find that it is one of the birds calling. He has had electricians come to the house and think someone was inside when one of the birds started talking.

Many birds that are not true or typical parrots but are classified in the scientific grouping known as the parrot family can speak. Cockatoos can speak, although they are more appreciated for their crests and their ability to whistle. Macaws can also be taught a few phrases. But of all the members of the parrot family (there are over 300 species), those parrots which can talk are the ones most widely kept, even when they are relatively poor speakers like budgies and cockatiels. African Greys can learn to recite long sentences and poetry. Not only will they pick up sounds on their own, but they will regroup them into different word-sound combinations. They possess what appears to be the power of association, the capacity to connect an object with a particular sound or phrase. There is almost no end to the vocabulary a good Grey can develop in time. Throughout history, talking parrots have been prized as household members because they continuously amuse their owners with their talking ability.

Parrots as Pets

Taming wild parrots, before the twentieth century, usually meant beating them with a stick until they learned. This was the punishment prescribed in the days of the Roman Empire to be used when a bird would not talk. Abuse of this nature persisted even into the nineteenth century and was thought to be the proper way to tame a bird. The bird was thought not to suffer, because its head was believed to be as hard as its beak. Small wonder that such birds did not breed! Today bird keepers are more informed and are usually spared the months of patience that it takes to properly tame a wild bird. I should clarify that by saying that most birds imported for sale are under a year old; older birds are extremely hard to tame. Occasionally wild, untamed parrots called "broncos" can be found, though never for sale commercially. Broncos can be very vicious, and their bite will surely break the skin. To tame these birds requires that they be isolated and glove-handled for months, and the wings are often wet down or clipped to keep them still.

Parrots come from South America, Asia, Australia and Africa. More species live in South America than in Asia, and Africa has the fewest. Interestingly enough, many of the parrots which are widely loved as pets are great nuisances in their homelands. The African Grey, as well as many of the Amazons, consumes planted seed, much to the

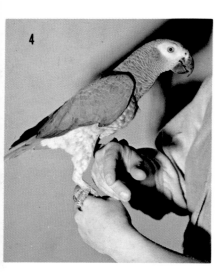
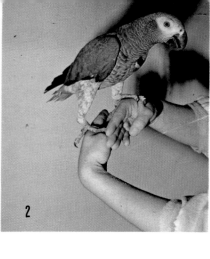

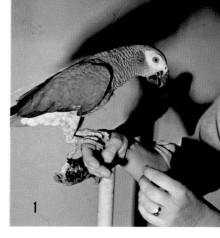
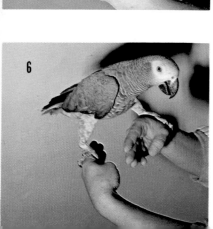

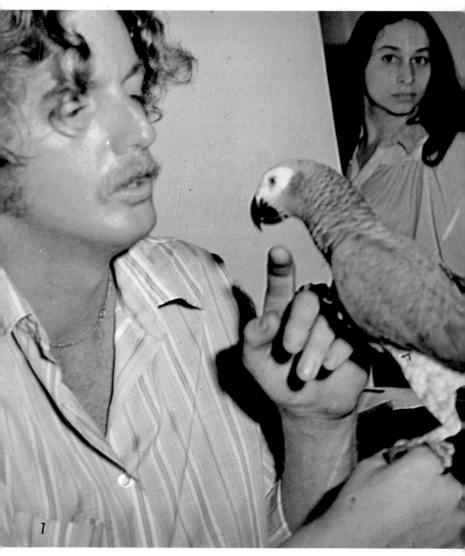

7

You cannot properly train a bird that is not tame. Taming requires constantly handling the African Grey. If your African Grey is caged, this same handling can be a good exercise. The photographs (1 through 6) on the facing page show step-by-step handling that will develop a rapport between the bird and its handler as well as provide exercise. While training the bird to speak (7) be sure that you are alone and there is no distraction. Photos by Dr. Herbert R. Axelrod.

15

dismay of the local inhabitants. Until modern times Greys were trapped and eaten by the natives, and now they are caught for sale abroad. Usually the birds are stolen from the nest and hand-raised or caught with bird lime, a sticky substance made from the bark of the holly tree. This black substance is smeared on tree branches in a location where the birds are known to roost. When the bird alights it is soon stuck to the tree limb and is easily caught. This is a more humane method than catching them by hand or with a net.

Sometimes, a prospective bird owner may come upon an African Grey that has either its flight feathers clipped or its tail plucked. Neither of these conditions detracts from the worth of the bird, and both will return when the bird molts. Clipping the wings is used to keep the bird docile for importation. The bright red tail feathers of the Grey are often pulled by the natives, who catch the birds and later sell the feathers.

African Greys are much sought after as cage birds. They are affectionate and long-lived, and their speaking ability sets them apart from the budgerigar and canary. The prospective bird keeper should always remember, however, that the bird he buys differs considerably in personality from the wild bird in its native habitat.

Scientific Classification

The parrot family, Psittacidae, is a very large family that comprises six subfamilies. Many of the birds are not even commonly called parrots, instead having names like conures, budgies and lovebirds, but nonetheless they are all classified as members of the parrot family. The largest members of the family are the long-tailed macaws of South America that can be 40 inches high. Macaws belong to the

To capture an escaped bird you can use a net or a towel. Do not wrap the towel (1) around the bird. The bird's head will protrude, and it can still bite! Approach it from the front (2), this will stop it from running away. Then drop the towel (3) over the bird's head and whole body. This, of course, assumes the bird has had its wings clipped and cannot fly. Photos by Dr. Herbert R. Axelrod.

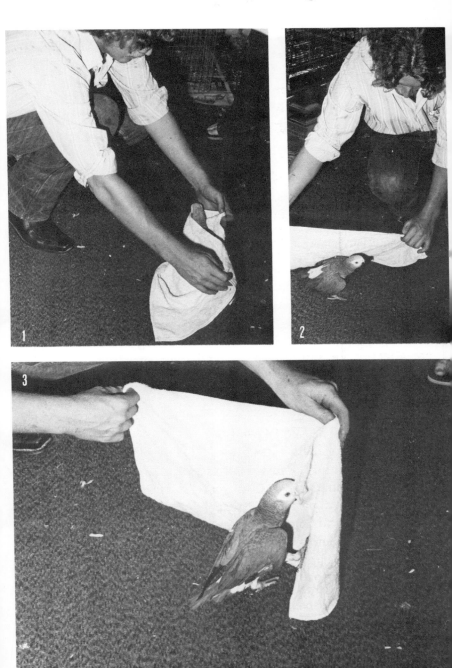

TRAINING YOUR AFRICAN GREY TO SPEAK PHRASES requires constant effort. You should handle the bird and have it relax with your usual exercises (1) and (2). Then introduce the phrase slowly and clearly. (3) Keep repeating the phrase over and over again until (4) the bird loses interest and wants to play again. Photos by Dr. Herbert R. Axelrod.

An African Grey on a "natural" perch. Unfortunately the birds soon chew these softwood perches to bits. Photo by Harry Lacey.

subfamily Psittacinae, as do lovebirds and the African Grey. The smallest members of the parrot family are the pygmy parrots of New Guinea, which belong in the subfamily Micropsittinae; these parrots are less than four inches in length. Other members of the parrot family include such diverse birds as lories and lorikeets, cockatoos, rosellas and grass parakeets.

These birds might not seem to have much in common, but they possess traits that all parrots share. Members of the parrot family have large, rounded, hooked beaks. They have large round heads and short necks, and their body is compact. Their feet are very specialized, with two toes in front and two behind, and the birds are agile in their use of them. They are usually forest-dwellers that live in trees. Their tongue is fleshy, the upper mandible of their hooked beak is movable, and many of them are nut and fruit eaters.

With some exceptions, parrots live in feeding flocks and nest in trees. The rock grass parakeet nests in rock hollows instead of trees, and the quaker parakeet lives in close-knit colonies instead of loose flocks, but most parrots share the above-mentioned traits. Additionally, parrots lay eggs that are white and rather round in shape, with clutches numbering from a single egg to eight.

On the facing page is a Galah, *Eolophus roseicapillus*. This bird makes a fine pet. Note the millet spray at its feet. The small bird to the left is a Turquoisine Grass Parakeet, *Neophema pulchella*. Photos by Harry Lacey.

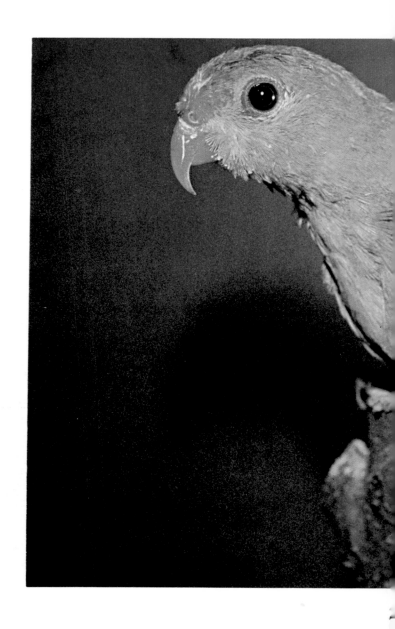

This Philippine Hanging Parrot (female) is as tiny as a canary. Its bill is typical for parrots, though sharp and dainty, showing the bird to be a fruit-eating species. Photo by Dr. Matthew Vriends.

A list of the subfamilies follows:

Subfamily Strigopinae: One species, *Stigops habroptilus,* the kakapo. This is a nocturnal bird that lives in New Zealand and is nearly extinct. It bears a superficial resemblance to owls because the facial feathers form a disk about the eyes.

Subfamily Nestorinae: The two species, the kea *(Nestor notabilis)* and the kaka *(Nestor meridionalis),* are both from New Zealand. They have long pointed beaks and are

The Eastern Rosella, *Platycercus eximius eximius,* from Australia. Photo by Harry Lacey.

known to kill sheep by pecking into the animal's flesh and eating the fat as well as the kidneys.

Subfamily Micropsittinae: The pygmy parrots, already mentioned, feed upon fungi growing at the base of trees. They are found only in New Guinea and adjacent islands.

Subfamily Kakatoeinae: Contains 16 species of cockatoos. Cockatoos are well known aviary birds and have large, graceful, erectile crests. Cockatoos are as a rule noisy birds in the aviary.

Subfamily Loriinae: This subfamily contains the lories and the lorikeets. These are popular aviary birds but are difficult to keep because of their feeding requirements. They feed mainly on pollen and honey which they suck up with their brush-like tongue. They are distributed throughout Indonesia, New Guinea and the Australian regions.

Subfamily Psittacinae: This subfamily contains all of the typical parrots, parrotlets, lovebirds, macaws, parakeets and conures. The African Grey and the Amazons belong to this very large subfamily.

The subfamilies aviculturists, members of the bird fancy and bird keepers are interested in are the Loriinae, Kakatoeinae and Psittacinae.

The subfamily Psittacinae contains 50 genera. The African Grey is the only species in the genus *Psittacus;* its specific name is *Psittacus erithacus.* Usually when naming a bird only the name of the genus and the name of the species are given, but this genus contains three subspecies: the "true" African Grey, *Psittacus erithacus erithacus;* the Timneh parrot, *Psittacus erithacus timneh;* and *Psittacus erithacus princeps.* The subspecies *princeps* is found only on two small islands off Africa and is probably not worth recognizing, but the Timneh parrot is fairly distinct, with a reddish brown instead of bright red tail and two white patches on the sides of the beak. The Timneh parrot is found only to the west of the true African Grey, in southern Guinea, Sierra Leone, Liberia and western Ivory Coast.

Mueller-Schmida's photograph of an African Grey. Compare this to the painting taken from Greene's book *Parrots in Captivity.*

The African Grey

Physical Characteristics

The adult male African Grey is roughly the same size as a pigeon, being about 14 or 15 inches in length; the female is smaller. An interesting characteristic of the young is that

the eyes change color as the bird grows into an adult. Under a year of age the bird's eyes are black, then they turn to gray, and eventually, when the bird has reached the adult stage, the eye color will be yellowish. The eye color of adults varies from pale yellow to yellowish white. Greys are slow to reach maturity; hens seldom lay eggs until past their third year.

The color of the African Grey is ash gray. The facial area is bare around the eyes, whitish in color and extends past the forehead, flaring backward past the eyes. The flight feathers are a darker gray, but when the wings are spread the middle and lower parts of the back can be seen to be grayish white. The breast feathers are tipped with white and overlap one another to give the bird a scalloped appearance, as if it were wearing a suit of chain mail.

The tail in adults is bright red, but in immatures the tail is a dark red above, with the under tail-coverts dark red and tinged with gray. The tail will change to a bright red after the first molt. A reddish coloration may be visible in various locations on the body besides the chest, even on the head, back and wings.

The legs and feet are black. In the immatures the feet are smooth, but in the older birds they are scaly. The bill is shiny black.

Distribution and Habits

The true African Grey is found in equatorial Africa from the Ivory Coast to Angola and inland to Kenya and Tanzania. They travel in flocks and when traveling by day make screeching and whistling noises. They also roost in flocks that may number into the hundreds. They are long-lived, even in captivity, with a record life-span for a bird in captivity of over 70 years. Normally they live from 20-25 years.

In the wild they are shy and suspicious and will fly away at the approach of an intruder. As already mentioned, they are farm pests and swoop down on cultivated grain crops. They are temperamental birds in captivity but are capable of great loyalty.

Greys are infrequent bathers and do not like being sprayed with water. Most birds emit an oil when they preen themselves and, by spreading it through their wings, leave their feathers with a glossy look. Greys are "dry-oil" birds that produce a powdery substance when they preen.

During the day Greys fly in flocks searching for fruit trees. They particularly like oil palm nuts, but will eat many other kinds of seeds. In captivity they will eat hard-boiled eggs, white bread soaked in milk, some hemp, canary seed, cooked potatoes and corn, as well as quantities of sunflower seeds, buckwheat, barley, oats, wheat, millet, rice (especially paddy), sorghum, and peanuts.

Breeding in nature takes place from July to September, depending on locality. The nest is usually a deep hole high up in a tree. The hen will lay from three to five eggs. They breed as a flock, but there is a difference of opinion as to whether they will nest in the same tree or not. I have read one source that stated that the birds will rarely, if ever, breed in the same tree occupied by another Grey. Another source reported that two or three pairs are likely to be seen together, occupying nesting holes in the same tree.

These birds have few natural enemies other than man. Their principal enemy is the falcon-like kite *Milvus parasitus,* which is about 22 inches in length and has a yellowish beak; kites are well-known scavengers. Another enemy is the palm vulture, *Gypohierax angolensis,* which is also called the vulture eagle.

African Greys occupy many coastal islands in the area called the Gold Coast. Prince's Island, also called Principe, is so overstocked with Greys that it is often called "The Paradise of the Grey Parrots." A subspecies of African Grey, *P.e. princeps,* has been described from this island, where the birds hold such dominion that they chase in-

The view above was taken in West Africa. It shows a typical habitat of the African Grey Parrot, with plenty of water, trees and grasses. The range of the African Grey is rather large, extending from the Ivory Coast to Angola and across the continent to Kenya and Tanzania. On the facing page is a typical Eastern Rosella, *Platycercus eximius eximius.* Compare this color photo to the black and white photo on page 24 so that you can evaluate the advantage color printing has made in the public's appreciation of parrots. Photos by Dr. Herbert R. Axelrod.

Since 1952, *Tropical Fish Hobbyist* has been the source of accurate, up-to-the-minute, and fascinating information on every facet of the aquarium hobby. Join the more than 50,000 devoted readers world-wide who wouldn't miss a single issue.

Subscribe right now so you don't miss a single copy!

Return To:
Tropical Fish Hobbyist, P.O. Box 427, Neptune, NJ 07753-0427

YES! Please enter my subscription to *Tropical Fish Hobbyist*.
Payment for the length I've selected is enclosed. U.S. funds only.

CHECK ONE:	☐ 1 year-$30	☐ 2 years-$55	☐ 3 years-$75	☐ 5 years-$120
	12 ISSUES	24 ISSUES	36 ISSUES	60 ISSUES

(Please allow 4-6 weeks for your subscription to start.) *Prices subject to change without notice*

☐ LIFETIME SUBSCRIPTION (max 30 Years) $495
☐ SAMPLE ISSUE $3.50
☐ GIFT SUBSCRIPTION. Please send a card announcing this gift. I would like the card to read: _____
☐ I don't want to subscribe right now, but I'd like to have one of your FREE catalogs listing books about pets. Please send catalog to:

SHIP TO:
Name _____
Street _____ Apt. No. _____
City _____ State _____ Zip _____
U.S. Funds Only. Canada add $11.00 per year; Foreign add $16.00 per year.
Charge my: ☐ VISA ☐ MASTER CHARGE ☐ PAYMENT ENCLOSED

Card Number _____ Expiration Date _____

Cardholder's Name (if different from "Ship to":) _____

Cardholder's Address (if different from "Ship to":) _____

Cardholder's Signature _____

...From T.F.H., the world's largest publisher of bird books, a new bird magazine for birdkeepers all over the world...

CAGED BIRD HOBBYIST
IS FOR EVERYONE
WHO LOVES BIRDS.

CAGED BIRD HOBBYIST
IS PACKED WITH VALUABLE
INFORMATION SHOWING HOW
TO FEED, HOUSE, TRAIN AND CARE
FOR ALL TYPES OF BIRDS.

Subscribe right now so you don't miss a single copy!

SM-316

Return to:
CAGED BIRD HOBBYIST, P.O. Box 427, Neptune, NJ 07753-0427

YES! Please enter my subscription to **CAGED BIRD HOBBYIST**. Payment for the number of issues I've selected is enclosed. *U.S. funds only.

CHECK ONE:	☐ 4 Issues	$9.00
	☐ 12 Issues for the Price of 10	25.00
	☐ 1 Sample Issue	3.00

☐ Gift Subscription. Please send a card announcing this gift.   PRICES SUBJECT TO CHANGE
I would like the card to read _____

☐ I don't want to subscribe right now, but, I'd like to receive one of your FREE catalogs listing books about pets. Please send the catalog to:

SHIP TO:
Name _____ Phone ( ) _____
Street _____
City _____ State _____ Zip _____

U.S. Funds Only. Canada, add $1.00 per issue; Foreign, add $1.50 per issue.

Charge my: ☐ VISA   ☐ MASTER CHARGE   ☐ PAYMENT ENCLOSED

Card Number _____ Expiration Date _____

Cardholder's Name (if different from "Ship to:") _____

Cardholder's Address (if different from "Ship to:") _____

Please allow 4–6 weeks for your subscription to start.   Cardholder's Signature

Like other intelligent animals, African Greys are inquisitive, always poking and exploring the world around them. In this they are aided by their four-toed feet, which enable them to grasp and hold objects for close examination. Photo by Mueller-Schmida.

←

Two views of a cage showing the attachment of feed and water cups and cuttlebone. The cups are easily refillable without having to put your hand into the cage, thereby disturbing the bird. Simply unlatch the cups, replenish the supply, slide the cups back in and relatch them. The cuttlebone (above cups in lower photo) is securely attached inside the cage but also is removable from the outside. Photos by Dr. Herbert R. Axelrod.

truders away. Interestingly enough, St. Thomas Island, neighboring Principe, is dominated by kites, and not a single Grey is to be found on the island.

Owners of African Greys have reported that the bird is a feather plucker. This may simply be normal preening, which is usually quite vigorous. During preening the bird may spend as much as 15 minutes cleaning off dust and dirt and loose down. Even in captivity it will preen for a long time, and, due to the pressure exerted, large feathers may fall out. However, sometimes the Grey and other parrots may be engaging in what is called "displacement preening." This is a nervous habit found only among caged birds. Although it is a form of nervous release, if persistent enough it can lead to actual plucking and the mutilation of good feathers. There is no cure except to try and occupy the bird's mind.

History

The African Grey has a long history. King Solomon is known to have kept birds caught in Africa, and many people think they were African Greys. At that time all parrot-like birds were called parrots; in any case, there is no mention of the bird's common name.

King Henry VIII is well known to have kept an African Grey, while the oldest known stuffed bird is an African Grey. This bird was kept by the beautiful Duchess of Richmond and Lennox, in England, who was known as "La Belle Stuart." At her death in 1660, she left plans to have the bird stuffed, and the bird, named the "Effigie," can be seen today in the Norman Undercroft Museum at Westminster Abbey in England. The bird was nearly forty when it died.

No one knows when the first parrot was brought to Europe, although some historians fix the first time by a reference made in 1455 to a "Senegal Parrot," though this parrot may well have been a Grey. In any case, the sailors who traveled the Gold Coast were familiar with the Grey and its peculiar shriek. The Portuguese named the bird the "jaco," for that is what the shrieking sounded like to them. Greys also make a "growling" sound that may be disturbing to someone who has never owned one. This is nothing to be alarmed about; it is just one of the bird's repertoire of sounds.

Greys have always been popular birds because of their ability to talk. Yet, though kept so long by aviculturists, breeding results are scarce. This is due in part to the problem of sexing the birds. The first recorded breeding of two African Greys in England was in 1945 by the well known aviculturist E.J. Boosey. Boosey bred birds in London for over forty years, and for his efforts he was awarded a medal by the Avicultural Society.

Finding a true pair of Greys has always made breeding difficult. Even dealers who import hundreds of Greys and have an eye for what is a male and what is a female are often misled. When they do post-mortems on birds that die, they frequently find that a bird supposed to be a female was a male and vice-versa.

Parrots in general have a long association with man. In the days of the Roman Empire their value was more than that of a slave, undoubtedly due to the difficulty of obtaining a parrot; Alexander the Great and Nero were parrot fanciers. In India parrots were neither caught nor eaten, being revered for their ability to talk.

Training your African Grey is different from taming it. Your African Grey (see photo to the left) should be tame enough to grasp things (food) from your finger. You might not be able to hold the bird (see below) and fondle it immediately, but it is only a matter of time. . .the time you want to put in. Photos by Dr. Herbert R. Axelrod.

Training

Buying an African Grey

As already mentioned, parrots are tamed before being sold commercially. Even an experienced aviarist may not be able to tame a bronco, and the best a prospective bird owner can do is to purchase his bird from a reliable pet shop owner or inspect the bird himself if buying from a bird breeder. This latter situation is due to the difficulty in breeding Greys. A wild Grey will try to bite and will be very much disturbed by the presence of humans.

The feet of the bird should be examined for missing toes. When standing, the bird should grasp its perch firmly and the wings should not droop but be closely held to the body. Do not be disturbed if the bird growls, as this is a characteristic of the Grey. The bird should not appear sick; the eyes should not be runny, and the bird should not have its

feathers puffed up around its body. Puffed up feathers are indications of a sick bird trying to maintain its body heat. Greys are more susceptible than Amazons to quick-killing diseases. A bird may be healthy on Monday and dead on Friday. This, unfortunately, is one of the hazards of buying birds.

Bringing the bird home usually presents few problems unless the outside temperature is considerably below 65 °F. The pet shop will often provide a carrying cage if the owner has not yet purchased a regular cage.

Training

The "shotgun" method is especially to be avoided with a talking bird like the Grey. The new owner in his zeal tries to teach the bird to talk in a week. This is very trying on the bird and usually ends with a feeling of distrust in both owner and bird. The Grey in particular is a high-strung animal and reacts to stress.

Training the Grey will take from two weeks to over six months. The first object is to hand-train it to the point where it accepts the owner's hand as a friendly force. African Greys have an instinctive fear of a man's hand, as it is usually synonymous with captivity. Spend 15 minutes a day and no more with the hand inside the cage door. The growling is a reaction of fright, but the owner should not desist in his efforts until the training period is over.

A bird's reaction to fright can be seen in the eyes. The pupils will contract and widen, and the feathers on the neck rise, much like the hackles of a dog. Dr. Matthew M. Vriends, whose experiences with breeding these birds will be discussed in a later chapter, says that some Greys are very temperamental. Some birds may be nasty for days, in which case the owner will have to gauge his appearances accordingly.

Greys do bite. However, unlike some other parrots, they do not hold on. Biting is usually not a problem, luckily.

Mishandling, teasing and unfamiliarity are causes of biting, and these can all be cured with proper training. If they bite you and break the skin, a little Mercurochrome should take care of it.

Also to be avoided are introducing the birds to strangers during training and even letting the other members of the household become too familiar. A basic rule is one parrot, one teacher. It may be best to mention here that the old chestnut about cutting out or splitting a parrot's tongue to enable it to talk sooner or with a larger vocabulary is a grave misstatement of fact and is never to be done.

Gradually the bird should be induced to perch upon the owner's hand and arm. This may demand much patience and attention on the part of the owner. The bird will be afraid at first, but if done with no one nearby it will eventually perch. If the bird is standing on its perch, place the forefinger or a rod underneath the breast close to the legs to induce it to perch. If the bird becomes afraid and slides away, the lesson should be discontinued until later. These lessons are not haphazard, and eventually your parrot will become so tame it will eat out of your hand.

Gradually the bird is taken out of the cage and familiarized with the room. The bird will take to the air more than once unless its wings have been clipped. These are minor mishaps, for eventually it will learn to trust the hand rather than its instincts. An escaped bird should be retrieved with a net so as not to damage the wings. A simple butterfly net will suffice or a special bird net can be bought.

During this initial training period the owner should attend to the bird's food and water, and the other household members should visit sparingly until the pet has accustomed itself to its new environment. Eventually it will wake with the household, eat with them and be friendly to all.

With the parrot out of its cage, it should be introduced to an out-of-the-cage perch. There are many kinds, some with perches on the top of the cage itself and others just stands with a perch on top. A word of caution: some newly imported birds have their flight feathers clipped, in which case they should be kept from elevated positions, because should they fall they may damage their breastbone. A bird with its wings clipped will not balance easily on its perch. You should ask your pet shop owner if the bird's wings have been clipped if you have any doubt.

One final word on training: the best way to hold a bird is to grasp it with one hand, the fingers enclosing the feathers in such a way that the bird cannot pry them loose to flap. Hold the bird loosely, without suffocating it; the fingers and thumb are placed at the sides of the head, under the eyes, so that the bird, with its supple neck, can not bite the fingers.

Teaching to Talk

Teaching a parrot to talk can be a hit-and-miss proposition. A lot depends on both bird and teacher. One important factor is whether the bird has been trained properly. Obviously the shotgun method referred to earlier will do more damage than harm. Another factor depends on the surroundings of the bird. If a young bird has been reared in the presence of too many other parrots, its talking ability will suffer. Parrots that are kept in an aviary do not talk as well as those kept in the home and individually trained. Also, if another bird is present during training, the two will be more interested in each other than in learning to talk.

A simple phrase or word should be used at first and repeated until the parrot understands that this is a form of communication. Of course bombarding the parrot with long sentences and poetry at the start will be worse than useless. Teaching a bird to recite many things from memory is really an arduous task. If the bird has been properly trained, the owner will be surprised to find that his Grey will talk "like crazy." At least that is the way most owners of African Greys describe the bird's talking, once they start.

When a bird talks it is imitating the speaker and most likely has no comprehension of the words themselves, unless it can associate them with a particular object or action. Since food goes so well with training a bird, it may be best to teach it the word for a food like an apple. The time-worn phrase "Polly wants a cracker" has a sound basis behind it.

While the time taken for a bird to talk may vary considerably (I have read of one bird owner who needed eight months to teach a parrot its name), once the bird learns to talk it will master a vocabulary in no time. Don't be discouraged if teaching a bird to talk takes many months . . . it will be well worth the effort. For a more comprehensive treatment of training a bird see *Taming and Training Budgerigars* by Cessa Feyerabend and Dr. Matthew Vriends.

Toys

Besides the amusement they provide for the owner and the bird, toys in the cage satisfy a real need, especially as far as parrots are prone to nervousness which can lead to premature molting and displacement preening. The main reason for this is that the bird is basically wild and will never entirely get used to living in a cage. Additionally, even in a large aviary they will not get the exercise they are accustomed to. To combat this nervousness the owner should experiment with mirrors, bells and ladders. Good toys are not dangerous and can only be considered as a plus on the part of the bird keeper.

When you buy a cage it still must be fitted with cups for food and water, and "treats" like millet spray and cuttlebone (above) must be added. Fancy cages are best and cheapest in the long run, but a homemade cage (see below) may be satisfactory for a short period of time. Homemade cages may rust, or the bird can chew itself out. Photos by Dr. Herbert R. Axelrod.

Cage and Aviary

Cage

Generally parrots, especially the larger members of the parrot family such as the Amazons and macaws, are best kept in an aviary. The smaller members live adequately in a cage. One of the main advantages of an aviary is that it allows the bird to exercise.

The most suitable site for a parrot cage is a well lighted corner of the room that is free from drafts. The temperature in the room should not go below 65°F. at night. The Grey is a tropical bird, but quite hardy. If the cage is kept in the basement, the circulation of gas or oil fumes should be inspected so as not to be inhaled by the bird. Fumes are definitely injurious when inhaled over a long period.

Greys need a large cage. A recommended size is three feet in length, two feet in width and two feet high. This is larger than is absolutely required, but the extra space will be appreciated by the parrot. The placement of the perches should allow enough head and wing room for flapping and preening.

Many kinds of cages are available, ranging from the ornate to the simple. It's a matter of taste and budget. Most cages, however, are made from stainless steel, which is a better metal than brass, which tarnishes. On the bottom is a sliding tray that greatly facilitates cleaning. If the parrot must be removed during cleaning and another cage is not handy, place the bird in a cardboard box or have someone hold it. This, of course, is only necessary if the bird has not been trained.

Sometimes the cage bars are painted. If the owner does the painting, he should be sure to use a non-toxic paint. Paint chips, and the parrot is a chewer that may inadvertently swallow some of the chips.

The Aviary

The aviary is used for keeping a multitude of birds. The prime considerations in buying or building an aviary are the available space and the number of birds to be housed. The aviculturist should always pay close attention to his selection of birds, because many species are territorial and others are pugnacious. In the wild the African Grey is known to be territorial when traveling in flocks, and they will chase away intruders.

In a small aviary it would not be advisable to house more than four Greys as they are apt to take up more than their share of the room available. This should not deter you from housing one or two in a small aviary, more in a larger aviary of thirty birds or more. Greys get along with other parrots such as lovebirds, conures and budgerigars.

The single disadvantage of keeping an African Grey in an

aviary is that it will probably not learn to talk. However, the bird will most likely live longer because of the exercise it will get, and also birds are more likely to breed if kept in an aviary. For the bird owners, birds can be shown to visitors without disturbing the birds.

The aviary has two sections: the shelter or birdhouse and the flight. The latter is a wire enclosure usually four to five times larger than the shelter to which it is attached. The floor of the flight is usually made of cement or hardwood. Bare earth is sometimes used but presents problems. The ground may have to be dug over every few months, limed and returfed for cleanliness. The advantage of cement is that the aviculturist can hose down the flight. Often wire netting is placed a few inches above the floor; this is to keep the birds from walking on their own dung and to make entry more difficult for nighttime predators.

Some aviculturists insist on a small flight section. The reason they give for this is that fledglings are apt to injure themselves in a large flight area by flying into the wire, and that this danger is reduced by shortening the length of the flight. This is true, but the problem can be dealt with without having to reduce the length of the flight. One method is to line the floor with branches and grassy foliage. Young birds fly not only to test their wings but to look for a place to hide. This branch method works well with grass parakeets. Another method is to cover the wire netting with another netting of nylon or cloth during the months that the new fledglings are learning to fly. In any case, the purpose of the flight is for exercising; by building a short flight the builder is defeating its purpose.

The shelter is often a converted shed, garage, or greenhouse. It can be built from scratch or purchased, and many types of small indoor aviaries are available. The shelter is usually made of wood and has a cement floor. If living in a humid climate the use of a dehumidifier will help in controlling moisture; the single disadvantage of cement is that it gives off and holds moisture. Some shelters are made of glass, but this must be lined with some kind of netting or the birds will fly into it.

The roof of the shelter is usually made of shingles, sheet metal or tile. It is sloped for diverting rainfall and is ventilated by drilling ducts near the roof, with wire covering them to keep the parrots inside and predators outside. Lighting and heating are added and a light may be placed outside to keep dangerous animals away. Weasels, mice, raccoons and stray cats are really a great nuisance, as many aviculturists can testify. One bad night and a bird keeper can be completely wiped out.

Many aviarists use half inch by half inch hardware cloth rather than aviary netting. Aviary netting is less expensive but of a lighter weight. It will keep out mice, but not weasels and other larger, sharp-toothed animals. A heavier aviary netting would be more widely spaced and might allow mice in. Incidentally, the cost of wire is determined by weight and size of mesh; the commonly used size for parakeets is one-half to three-quarter inch mesh. Mesh is often painted to avoid rusting and to increase visibility for the birds. This is fine, but lead-based paints are not to be used.

For the Grey, a good size of flight would be from 15 to 20 feet, with a height of about eight feet. The indoor aviaries already mentioned come in considerably smaller sizes, but for keeping one or two birds they serve admirably and are, in any case, better than a cage.

An African Grey cage ready for use. The cage door has a clasp lock, and there is sufficient seed and water. The tray is removable and has sand paper on the bottom. The cuttlebone is in place, a seed bell is hanging in the proper position. . .and the cage is made of sufficiently heavy wire to insure that the bird cannot chew through. Photo by Dr. Herbert R. Axelrod.

Many parrots are chewers. This is not dangerous, but it is possible for the bird to chew a hole big enough to escape, though generally it will be noticed before that happens. In some older aviaries where the wood is starting to rot or in a converted structure which might have loose boards, sheet metal can be used for patching.

Perches

Perches are more important than the average bird keeper realizes, especially when the length of time a bird spends on one is considered. Perches should be of varying thicknesses so that the parrot's feet will not cramp. In an aviary they should be placed close to the roof and spaced so that one bird will not defecate on another. Perches are located near the ceiling so that the birds will roost there if the bird keeper enters.

Natural branches and perches available commercially can both be used. Natural branches will have to be replaced periodically as the wood turns brittle. They may also be a problem if they have been sprayed with insecticides or have mites. Even a single mite may be the source of an infestation. For this reason I would recommend perches that have been brought from a pet store, as mites are a great nuisance. But whichever perch is chosen, should it become mite-invested, it must be burned.

Perches should neither be so small that the bird cannot grasp them nor so large that the bird cannot maintain its balance. A good size for perches is about two and a half to three inches for the African Grey.

You may hear of aviculturists who use perches situated near the floor. This is for birds that are ground-dwellers, such as grass parakeets. The idea is good but can be eliminated by the use of branches and grassy foliage situated on the floor, since most ground-dwellers are hiders. Only if a bird damages a wing should perches be installed close to the ground.

Drinking Facilities

Unlike some other parrots, African Greys drink and bathe infrequently, so they should adapt to any watering system. There are many kinds of drinkers, ranging from automatic drinking systems for the larger aviaries to a bowl or pie plate in the center of the aviary. Very few commercially purchased cages come without drinkers.

Those owners using a bowl or pie plate should know that eventually a crust of algae will form. One school of thought recommends that the algae should be left as the birds will receive added nutrients, particularly iodine. The algae should be scraped away every other week, as the risk of infecting the birds is far greater than the value of the nutrients.

Many aviaries are set up with a shower spray, as most birds like to bathe. The Grey will not stand around and be sprayed, and it will fly away in fright. This will mean an inconvenience for the bird owner, but should he decide to hose his birds down he can just remove his Greys or see to it that they do not get wet.

Feeders

The Grey is apt to take over a single feeder, so many should be provided. If the Grey, or any other bird for that matter, should become bossy over the feeder, the bird owner can construct smaller feeders. Feeders should not be so large that the parrot can stand on the seed, and the feeders should not be located near the water pan, as dripping water will cause the seed to become moldy.

If you look objectively at an African Grey you can tell from a distance that the bird is alert and healthy. The bird in the photograph to the left is obviously healthy. The bird below has a feather problem caused by a degeneration of the powder down feathers. Only the breast feathers are affected at this time. Photos by Harry Lacey.

Diseases

Birds are susceptible to a wide range of diseases. The purpose of this chapter is to familiarize bird owners with some of the more frequently encountered diseases and to list some of the symptoms and recommend advice and medications. If a bird should become sick, it is strongly recommended that it be taken to a veterinarian, even if the bird recovers. This is especially important in an aviary setting, where a contagious disease could wipe out an entire flock of foreign birds. Should a bird die it should be taken to a veterinarian for a post-mortem examination, usually

referred to as "posting." As a further reference on the subject of diseases see *Bird Diseases* by L. Arnall and I.F. Keymer, published by T.F.H. Publications.

A sick bird is readily identified. Sick birds refuse to fly and choose to sit in a corner of the cage. The feathers are fluffed up to preserve body heat. The eyes are closed or discharging fluid. Breathing may be irregular and the tail may be jerking up and down. Droppings are runny and may be stained with blood (which may be caused by a change in diet). If a bird exhibits any of these symptoms it should be removed from other birds until the cause of its behavior is discovered.

External diseases, like cankers and some tumors, are visible to the eye, as are some parasites. Mites and ticks can be a real nuisance in an aviary but are not lethal. Some of the more common parasites will be discussed with suggestions for dealing with them.

Acclimation

The African Grey is more susceptible to disease than other parrots, and sick Greys should be taken to a veterinarian as soon as possible. Amazons will linger for a week or longer upon contracting a disease, while Greys die suddenly. Part of the difference in susceptibility is due to the high-strung nature of the Grey. In any case, a sick Grey should be removed to a hospital cage at once, and as soon as it is convenient—preferably the next day—the bird should be taken to a doctor.

A rule of thumb for the aviarist is that a Grey should be isolated for three weeks to a month before introducing it to other birds. Birds that are brought into the United States are quarantined by law before they can be sold commercially. It will be found that African Greys being acclimatized settle down more rapidly if kept in a steady temperature of between 65°-75°F. By becoming acclimatized, the parrots adjust themselves to withstand without any noticeable ill-effects our very variable weather conditions; they can stand quite an appreciable amount of cold, providing they have their daylight hours lengthened artificially.

Hospital Cages

The first requirement of a sick bird is heat. Birds have a much higher metabolism than humans, with a body heat of 104°-105°F. Birds are more susceptible to fever than most other animals, and a bird that has its feathers puffed up is trying to preserve its body heat by using the dead-air space under the feathers for insulation. The hospital cage is a specially designed cage for isolating a bird and giving it more heat.

A hospital cage is usually made of steel and has a glass front. Inside is an insulating cloth. The heat source may be a light bulb or an infra-red lamp. The hospital cage is usually a temporary measure. As already mentioned, sick birds should be taken to a veterinarian soon after they become sick.

Colds

Colds are very common in tropical birds. They are caused by a virus that produces symptoms similar to those of a human cold. A runny nose, sneezing, coughing and sitting with feathers puffed up are symptoms of a cold.

The bird should be removed to a hospital cage with a temperature setting of 85°F. Epsom salts may be added to mineral water to clear congestion. The main problem with a cold is that the bird may contract pneumonia. Birds rarely die of a simple cold.

Diarrhea

Diarrhea is not a disease. It is simply a soft, watery bowel movement that can be due to an infection of the gut from eating contaminated food or drinking oily liquids. Usually the vent becomes wet and dirty.

Discontinue the feeding of green foods for awhile and place the bird in a warm room free from drafts. Placing the bird in a hospital cage is not necessary. If the condition does not clear up within a few days, take the bird to a veterinarian. Diarrhea is usually a symptom, not a disease; it can be caused by a change in diet resulting in stomach upset, but if persistent can be indicative of a variety of ailments such as a tumor in the kidney, liver damage or bacterial infection. Diarrhea, though not serious in itself, is not to be taken lightly.

Premature Molt

Birds molt once a year and often will molt out of season. However, in some birds the molt will be extended by excessive feather picking on the bird's part. In extreme cases the bird will pick out feathers to the point of leaving bald patches.

Problems with a bird engaging in excessive molting are often psychological. It is normal for a bird to want to scratch itself as the new pin feathers grow in; however, some birds, particularly parrots, engage in vigorous preening which can become so excessive as to be termed neurotic. A caged bird receives little exercise and does not take to confinement easily, being more familar with a wide-open forest. Besides plucking out good feathers, a caged bird may scratch its feet, bob its head and screech without reason. Outside of distracting the bird's attention and using cage toys, there is little that can be done.

Psittacosis

This disease received great notoriety in the 1930's, but today is so rare that only passing mention need be made of it. At one time it received a lot of attention because it is communicable to humans and not easily diagnosed. Psittacosis is caused by a virus *(Miyagawanella psittaci)*, and its symptoms resemble pneumonia. The disease can be diagnosed by a blood test and is easily cured by penicillin. With the advent of quarantine laws and better methods of shipment, this disease is now all but nonexistent.

Mouth Canker

Mouth cankers appear as a small whisker-like bud that grows around the bird's beak. Often it will fall off and a new bud will take its place.

A mouth canker can be a serious affliction. It often becomes painful to the point that the bird no longer eats and soon dies. Treating the canker with Mercurochrome daily will clean a canker, although it may take a week or longer. The skin around the beak may become blistered, in which case the treatment should be stopped until the blisters clear up.

Feather Cyst

When one or more undeveloped feathers fail to emerge from a feather follicle, a cyst may form. Cysts contain fluid and sometimes become infected. Opening and cleaning out the cyst can be done by the bird owner, but it is best done by a veterinarian since there is often heavy bleeding.

Foot problems

There are many foot disorders, but most of them can be eliminated by maintaining a clean cage. If the bird's feet become caked with mud and dirt, they should be soaked in luke-warm water and dried with cotton. Dettol can be added to the water to prevent infection. The condition called scaly feet is caused by a mite and appears as rough whitish lumps on the feet; if not taken care of, it can spread over the entire body. The mites can be killed by coating the feet with Vaseline, which will suffocate the mites.

Broken limbs

Amputation of a broken limb is not critical, and a parrot can survive with a minimum of discomfort (although mating may become impossible). A veterinarian should remove the limb, as the operation requires sterile conditions. If the fracture is not major, it can be set with a splint. A match or thin blade of wood can be used for a broken leg, but a wing fracture will almost always surely have to be set by a veterinarian because of the difficulty involved. When a bird is at rest the wing is held in a flexed or bent position.

Nails and Beak

Sometimes a section of the beak will break off if the bird flies into something or has a fight. The beak will grow back although it may be misshapen.

Trimming the nails and the beak can be done by the bird owner. Only the upper end of the nail is trimmed, as there is a vein that runs into the foot. This vein can be seen by holding the bird's foot up to a light. Cutting the beak is more difficult, as a vein also runs through the upper mandible and the bird's tongue may get in the way. The bird is also likely to struggle. Unless one has done trimming before, he should take the bird to a veterinarian.

Mites

Mites, luckily, are not killers, and usually they are easy to spot. Most species are blood suckers and if not eradicated may leave the birds anemic and susceptible to other diseases.

The red mite *(Dermanyssus)* is a common mite that is difficult to detect because it drops off the bird and hides during the day. It is called the "red" mite because it is usually gorged with blood after its nighttime feeding. The best way to check for this mite is to look in dark places in the aviary where the bird might hide. Look inside the nest boxes and the perches, under any tree limbs and in grassy foliage.

Mites that attack parrots are not easily discerned because the bird's scratching is often mistaken for a nervous habit such as displacement preening. By gently unfurling the bird's feathers the mites can be spotted. There are a number of powders that can be used after washing the bird thoroughly. Avoid DDT and lindane. Perches and other discardables should be burned.

Tapeworms

Tapeworms are difficult to diagnose, but once diagnosed are easily eradicated. The most effective cure is the use of doses of Kamal powder in the food.

Among the dangers of allowing your African Grey the freedom of the house is the possibility that the Grey will climb onto the cage of a bird protecting its nest. If the bird is aggressive it might well bite off the toe of the invading African Grey. Photo by Dr. Herbert R. Axelrod.

A nestful of baby African Greys. Though they are difficult to breed because they are so difficult to sex, it is not an impossibility. Generally speaking (see below) the male has a longer and larger head, but it might well take an expert to appreciate the differences.

Breeding

African Greys are extremely difficult birds to breed in captivity. They are temperamental and high-strung, and in the wild are flock birds that pair only to mate. Dr. Matthew M. Vriends, to whom the author is greatly indebted for material in this chapter, related an experience he had in Australia while trying to breed African Greys. He tried pairing a male with a young female. Dr. Vriends described

the female's reactions as strange: she started to shiver and remained in a corner. Several times she attacked the male when he came too close, but after a couple of days they seemed to settle down. One day the male was spied attempting to mount the female. He had placed one foot on the back of the female and was lifting the other foot, when, just at that moment, the female wiggled loose and bit him on the foot so that he tumbled off. Eventually the birds had to be separated.

Experiences like this are not uncommon, and I've heard of a persistent breeder who has been trying unsuccessfully to breed a pair for eight years.

Of course not all breeders are so unlucky, and Greys can be bred. Two problems with breeding African Greys are sexing the birds and obtaining a mature female. The female does not attain maturity for at least three years, meaning that a bird breeder may have to wait at least two years before he even begins, since most commercially obtained birds are about one year of age.

Sexing

The African Grey is especially difficult to sex. Generally the male is longer than the female and the head and beak of the male are noticeably larger. The eye shape is slightly different: the female's are smaller and more elliptical, while the male's are round. Another indicator is feeling the pelvic bones. The male's pelvic bones are closer together when compared to the female's, which must be wide enough to allow eggs to pass. These differences are of course more apparent if one has a pair to begin with.

Another method now being used in determining the sex of the bird is through a surgical incision made in the bird's side. This is a relatively simple affair and is the best way to truly determine the sex of the bird. An operation might strike some people as unnecessary, even cruel, but if the price of a pair of Greys is taken into account, then it is another matter. Additionally, there are some unscrupulous people in the world. Take the following example.

The African Grey is sometimes mistaken for the Australian roseate cockatoo *(Kakatoa roseicapilla roseicapilla).* I have read that this cockatoo is sometimes sold under the name Australian Grey parrot. Both birds are about the same size and both are grey with pink on the breast areas, though they are only vaguely similar in overall color. The differences between the two are even more apparent once they are acclimated in the house: the African Grey, though noisy and a pest in the wild, is a very tame bird and is not noisy, while the roseate cockatoo is well known for its shrieking. This is not mentioned to downgrade the roseate cockatoo as a cage bird (in fact, it is the second most widely kept of the cockatoos in captivity), but the African Grey is likely to cost considerably more.

Sexing birds is of great importance for bird breeders, and accuracy and honesty are not always guaranateed by word of mouth. While familiarity with the birds may not guarantee a true pair, it will help prevent buying the wrong bird.

A hen African Grey Parrot "seems" more delicate, with a shorter neck and smaller head. Photo by Mueller-Schmida.

Breeding in the Wild

In the wild, African Greys breed in late summer, and incubation lasts roughly a month. The best time to buy an African Grey in the United States is in the early part of the year; the birds are approximately six months old at this time.

The hen lays from two to four eggs. When the chicks hatch they are naked and blind but will have a covering of down within a week. Greys spend up to two months in the nest, and the hen continues feeding them, regurgitating a milky substance from her crop. The eggs measure roughly one and one-half inches long.

At the onset of breeding the female dances around the cock with her wings held low and her tail spread out. She usually engages in repeated up and down motions with her head. Generally, both male and female will feed the young. African Greys nest in tree hollows and generally do not build a nest. In captivity they sometimes lay eggs on the floor of the cage.

Breeding

Dr. Matthew M. Vriends was living in his native Holland in 1959 and was in contact with Mr. John Peursum, who lived in Ede, Holland. Mr. Peursum had a female African Grey in his possession at this time and fed it (in addition to seeds) vegetables, pieces of meat and bone marrow. In 1964 he bought a male who was five years old and then attempted breeding. The age of the female was 15 years.

He was successful in that the female dug a hole in the center of the aviary and deposited a couple of eggs. The eggs were fertile, but nothing happened. This was in September.

In November, the weather having gotten colder, Mr. Peursum moved the birds inside to a cage 3½ x 2¾ x 2 feet (100 x 80 x 60 cm). That December the hen laid three eggs within the first week. Dr. Vriends, who had been anxiously watching the progress of the birds, placed the eggs into a pigeon saucer. This turned out to be disagreeable to the hen, who had laid the eggs at the bottom of the cage. The saucer was removed and the eggs returned to the bottom of the cage. The hen resumed incubation, and 30 days after the first egg had been laid, it hatched. One other egg hatched, and the third proved to be sterile. The first chick had great difficulty getting out of its shell. Dr. Vriends reports that instead of attempting to break out of the egg by cracking the shell around the air-sac at the wide end, the chick attempted to make a break lengthwise in the egg. This vertical cut (from tip to tip) allowed air into the egg at a much quicker rate, drying up the membrane, thus making it more difficult for the chick to hatch. The male did not participate in the feeding of the young, but he did feed the hen, who in turn fed the young.

Nest Boxes

As can be seen from Dr. Vriends' experience, African Greys are fussy with their eggs and may choose to incubate them on the ground. Dr. Vriends says that breeding successes have been recorded using a beer barrel converted for nesting purposes and a tree stump with a hole drilled into it. The insides were lined with some straw, and the birds were not interfered with.

Egg Problems

Parrots, as well as other birds, suffer from a variety of egg problems. The most common are egg-binding and soft-shelled eggs. Both are usually caused by a deficiency in the diet, usually the absence of grit and greens.

The egg shell is not solid. While serving as a protective wall around the embryo, the shell is porous to let oxygen in and carbon dioxide out. The embryo would suffocate if the shell were not porous.

Egg-bound refers to a condition whereby the hen is unable to lay her eggs. A lack of calcium is the chief cause of egg-binding. Usually the hen displays her condition by leaving the nest and acting like a very sick bird, sitting in a corner with eyes closed and feathers fluffed up, or she will try vainly to expel the egg. Sometimes there is paralysis.

Let a veterinarian handle an egg-bound hen. If the egg is inadvertently broken, the hen will most likely perish. Experienced aviculturists can diagnose this condition by gently feeling the pelvic area for the egg. Sometimes both egg and hen can be rescued. An often recommended remedy is dropping some mineral oil into the vent.

A soft-shelled egg is just that, an egg with a very thin or incompletely formed shell. The hen will usually dispose of this herself. However, an examination should be conducted because sometimes this is an indication of a tumor.

KEEPING YOUR AFRICAN GREY HEALTHY might require a few additional supplies. (1) A cuttlefish bone to attach to the cage gives additional calcium, as does (2) a dietary supplement. (3) First aid products are always needed. (4) Sand paper for the cage bottom and sand-covered perch covers keep the birds' nails to a manageable size. Photos by Dr. Herbert R. Axelrod.

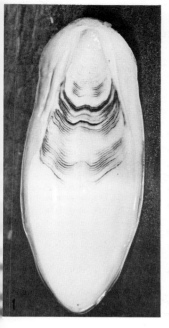

1

2

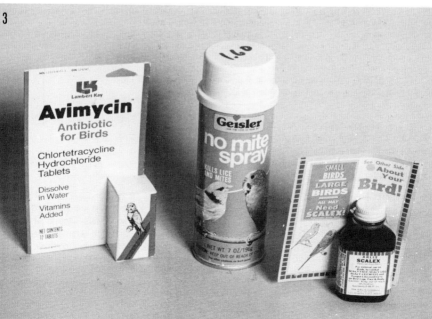

3

Wild African Greys that are not friendly can be spotted from a distance. They may hiss and scream, and their pupils are small as they talk. They bow and take a defensive position.

It is not a safe practice to train your African Grey to "kiss" you. They are still animals and would not be responsible if they were frightened by a barking dog or a stranger and bit through your lip! Photo by Sam Fehrenz.

Your African Grey Parrot can be trained to eat a variety of foods. If you intend to train your bird, it should be fed only by hand so that it can appreciate that you are his friend and a necessary part of life.

Food Requirements

Parrots have four basic food requirements: seeds, water, cuttlebone and grit. Two kinds of seed are required, oil and non-oil seed. Budgie mixtures contain non-oil seeds, and their nutritional value is determined by the composition and freshness of the seed. Canary seed has the highest protein content of the non-oil seeds, and a higher proportion of this seed will cost more.

To determine the freshness of your seed, germinate it. Place one hundred seeds on a piece of paper, wet them and leave them in a warm, airy place for two or three days. Sub-

Your African Grey Parrot needs a cage large enough for it to climb around and get exercise. Some cages have wires that are horizontal (not vertical as shown here). These horizontal wires make climbing easier. Perches (see facing page) should be of varying thicknesses so that the bird has the chance to exercise its toes. Photo above by Dr. Herbert Axelrod. Photo on the facing page by Sam Fehrenz.

tract the number of dead seeds to get an accurate count to determine freshness.

Parrots need oil seeds because they are rich in amino acids. Common oil seeds are sunflower, niger, maw and linseed. All seeds should be stored so that fresh air keeps them from spoiling. The seed should be kept in a porous bag and stirred by hand occasionally. No more than two or three pounds per bird should be purchased at a time.

Canary seed has elongated kernels. Millet is plump and round; the best type has cream-colored kernels. Dark yellow and red millets are also used.

Some birdowners mix their own seed. A common mixture used is four parts canary to two parts millet and one part oats. The seeds should be thoroughly mixed so that the bird eats enough canary seed. More oats should be added to the mixture if the bird is under a year old. Oats are fattening and needed more by a growing bird.

Birds eat all day long but take their main meal at night, filling their crops. The seed containers should be replenished before this time and discarded seed husks should be blown from the top of the seed containers.

Dr. Vriends says that a good seed mixture would be:

Buckwheat	10%
Barley	5
Oats	5
Canary seed	5
Corn	10
Rice (particularly paddy)	10
Sorghum	5
Wheat	10
Millet	10
Nuts (peanuts, almonds,)	5
Hemp	5
Sunflower seed	20

Offer these seeds in two different cups: one for the small and one for the large seeds, etc.

Sprouted Seed

Sprouting seed is the best way to ensure freshness and maximum nutritional value, but it is impractical unless a bird owner has a large aviary. Another disadvantage is that even when a preserving agent is used, the seed is wet and must be eaten within a shorter time than dry seeds.

The usual seed mixture is canary, proso millet and oats, germinated with a preserving agent. When the seed sprouts, the mixture is drained and placed in another container which has holes drilled into the bottom. The seed is watered down again until the sprouts are about an inch long, when they are fed to the birds. This whole process takes about three days.

Grit

Grit is used by a bird for grinding the seeds that are eaten. It serves as the bird's teeth and, in the wild, is usually sand and small pebbles. Commercial grit has crushed granite as a base and contains minerals such as sulphur, calcium and phosphorus.

For larger aviaries grit can be purchased in bulk and stored. To the grit can be added crushed egg shell which has been boiled for twenty minutes to kill salmonella bacteria. Another additive is crushed oyster shell.

The grit container should be checked every week and replenished frequently. Birds are very selective when it comes to grit and will not eat much of the grit offered them.

Cuttlebone

Cuttlebone is taken from the cuttlefish (a type of squid) and is composed mostly of calcium carbonate. By biting on it the bird helps keep its beak in trim as well as consuming calcium. A common budgie cuttlebone may be too soft, as the African Grey is a hard chewer. Tougher cuttlebones are available commercially.

A closeup, enlarged view of blood feathers in the wing of an African Grey. Blood feathers, or pin feathers, are feathers still in the process of growing: the developed feather emerges from its sheath, which eventually disintegrates. As the sheath contains pulp and a blood supply, it will bleed if cut. When trimming the feathers of the wing, avoid clipping any blood feathers present. Photo by Dr. Herbert R. Axelrod.

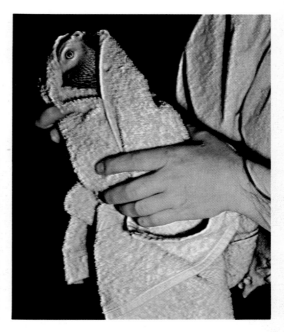

In order to examine your bird, or to take it to see the veterinarian, you should wrap it carefully in a towel. It takes two people to do a proper wrapping job. One person should hold the bird's head and feet while the second person wraps the bird. Photos by Dr. Herbert R. Axelrod.

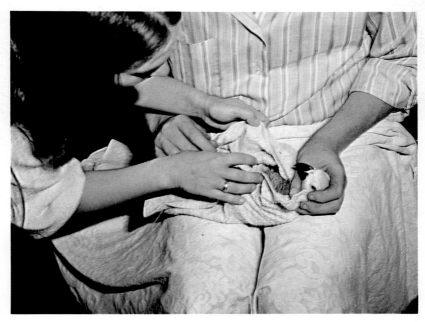

PARROT NECESSITIES include (1) Seed and treat cups. (2) Various kinds of seed for variety. (3) Cod liver oil supplement. (4) Vitamin supplement. (5) Fresh seeds used by farmers. (6) Sunflower and maize. (7) Honey stick treats. (8) Various kinds of water and treat cups.

When clipping the flight feathers of an African Grey Parrot, you need two people. One holds. . .the other cuts. The grip on the bird's head and feet must be firm and secure. Only the feathers on one wing need be cut. Photo by Dr. Herbert R. Axelrod.

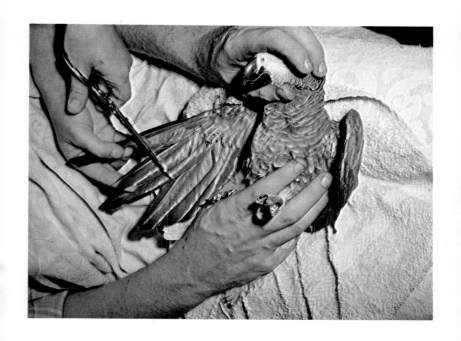

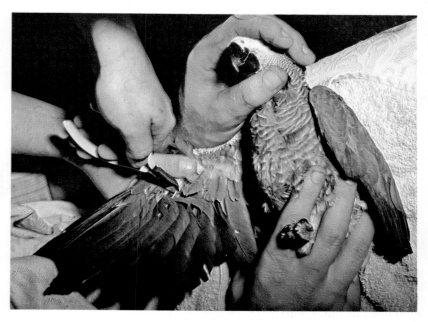

Greens

Greens are important for their nutritional value and for providing color for the birds. The African Grey, which drinks little, should be offered spinach, endive and chickweed for additional water. Chickweed is a low weed with star-like white flowers. This plant can be grown outside the house. Lettuce, though low in nutritional value, can be given. Fruits, too, should be given as a treat, as well as soaked bread. Sliced apples and orange sections will be eaten by the African Grey as well as small (5 inches) other fruits and willow twigs.

Cod-live Oil and Wheat Germ Oil

Neither of these oils is a must, but mixing a teaspoon into the bird's seed periodically will add many needed nutrients. It should not be mixed in stored seed but specially prepared in another bowl just before being given to the bird.

GERMINATING SEED. Use an aluminum pan and cover it with clear film (1) so you can see the stage of sprouting. First the seed must be poured into a strainer (2) and then soaked in a bowl of water. But you should gather everything you need (3) before you start. The seed must be fresh or it won't sprout. The seed in the strainer should be soaked (4) for 12 hours. Then the water should be changed (5), that's why the strainer is necessary. Before the seed is placed into the sprouting tray (6) it must be washed under running water (7) and soaked for an additional 12 to 24 hours. Photos by Dr. Herbert R. Axelrod.

2

3

4

5

6

7

81

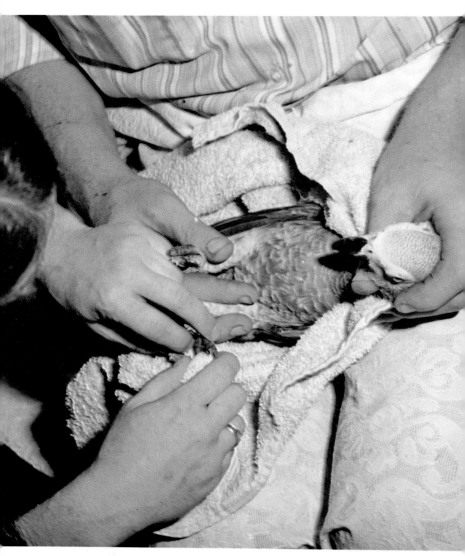

To cut your African Grey's claws requires two people. The person holding the bird must also isolate one foot (1) so that each claw can be examined by the person doing the cutting. The nails should be clipped with a special nail clipper available at your pet shop or a sharp wire cutter (2). Then the person holding the bird must assist in changing the grip to facilitate clipping the nails on the second foot. Note (3) that the bird is always held firmly in the holding person's lap. Photos by Dr. Herbert R. Axelrod.

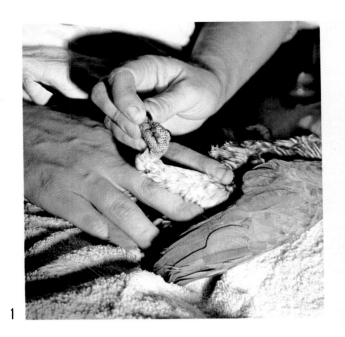

1

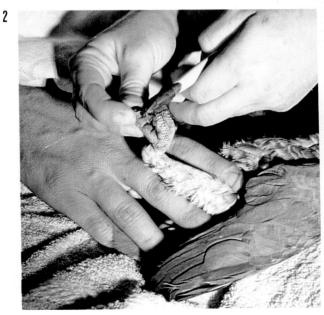

2

83

The Banksian Cockatoo is
a popular talking bird. But
it cannot compare in
popularity with the African
Grey (lower photo),
because the African Grey
is easier to tame and train.

Other Talking Parrots

Yellow-bellied Senegal parrot *(Poicephalus senegalus)*

The Senegal parrot is a short, rather stocky bird with a square tail. It is about 9 to 9½ inches in length. The tail and wings are green, and the lower breast and under tail-coverts are yellow. A brownish gray color covers the head. The eyes are yellow, and the bill is black.

The Senegal is found in the drier regions of West Africa in Senegal and Portuguese Guinea. They fly in small flocks numbering two dozen or so in the wild. Mischievous like the African Grey, they eat cultivated crops and fruit and are well known for eating the fruit of the monkey-bread tree. Nests are holes in large trees. The hen lays 3 to 4 eggs. The Senegal is an excellent cage bird and a talker, though it does not have the reputation of the African Grey.

Other popular talking parrots are (1) The Blue-fronted Amazon, *Amazona aestiva aestiva,* (2) The Yellow-crowned Amazon, *Amazona ochrocephala auropalliata,* (3) The Kea, *Nestor nobilis,* and (4) The Yellow-lored Amazon, *Amazona xantholora.* Photos by (1) Horst Mueller, (2,3) W. de Grahl, and (4) Dr. Herbert R. Axelrod.

Mexican Double Yellow Head *(Amazona ochrocephala oratrix)*

This parrot is sometimes called Levaillant's Amazon. The parrot is about 15 inches long and is a noisy bird but has an excellent record as a talker. The eyes are red and the beak white. This parrot gets its name from the spots of yellow in its head. The wings are tipped with red and blue and are red near the base. These birds often become so tame they can be left completely at liberty, although they vary tremendously in disposition. Often they will bite.

Yellow-naped Amazon *(Amazon ochrocephala auropalliata)*

Also incorrectly called the Panama parrot (which is *A.o. panamensis*), this is a very popular parrot in the United States and is possibly the best-selling large parrot. It is slightly larger than the Mexican double yellow head. The coloring is green with a paler green on the breast and head. This parrot gets its name from the yellow band on its nape. The wings are greenish blue on the flight feathers and pinkish red on the secondaries. It is possessive and generally sticks to one owner.

Yellow-fronted Amazon Parrot *(Amazona ochrocephala ochrocephala)*

Sometimes called the yellow-headed Amazon parrot, this bird has a basically green coloration; the feathers of the neck and mantle are yellow. The wings are beautifully laced with color: the bend of the wings is red; the secondary feathers are blue-black near the tip; and a bluish coloration extends throughout the wings.

This is an excellent talking bird, and some experts consider it to be the most intelligent of the Amazons. These parrots fly in large flocks and are a great nuisance to the farmers. Like many parrots, they are difficult to breed in captivity.

Blue-fronted Amazon Parrot *(Amazona aestiva)*

This parrot comes from Brazil. At one time in Europe, this parrot was the most commonly imported parrot, exceeding in numbers the African Grey. Like all of the Amazons, it is a splendid talker, but also a poor breeder. It is 14-15 inches in length. Sometimes it becomes so tame it can be left at liberty.

The coloration is mostly green. A band of blue extends across the forehead, the wings are tipped with blue and the feathers on the hindneck and mantle are edged with black. The eye is orange, and the legs and feet are gray.

Spectacled Amazon Parrot *(Amazona albifrons)*

This is a well known talker and is very popular in the United States. The first recorded breeding in the U.S.A. was in 1949. This parrot is sometimes called the white-fronted or white-breasted Amazon parrot.

The spectacled Amazon has a distribution along the Pacific coast of Mexico. The basic coloration is green. The bird gets its name from the white band on its forecrown. The feathers surrounding the eyes are red. The beak is pale yellow, and the legs and feet are grayish white. This bird is ten and one-half inches in length.

Yellow-lored Amazon Parrot *(Amazona xantholora)*

This parrot is similar to the spectacled Amazon parrot. The forehead and forecrown are white, and the basic coloration is green throughout. Around the eyes the feathers are red.The rest of the feathers are slightly edged with black, with a heavy black coloring on the neck, mantle and upper breast.

Less expensive talking parrots are (1) The Senegal Parrot, *Poicephalus senegalus,* (2) The Budgerigar, *Melopsittacus undulatus,* (3) The Yellow-naped Amazon, *Amazona ochrocephala auropalliata,* and (4) The Spectacled Amazon, *A. albifrons.* Photo by (1) Horst Mueller, (2) Bates and Busenbark, (3) Dr. Herbert R. Axelrod and (4) Horst Mueller.

Suggested Reading

The following T.F.H. Publications titles are available at pet shops everywhere.

PARROTS OF THE WORLD
By Joseph M. Forshaw
ISBN 0-87666-959-3
TFH PS-753

This book covers every species and subspecies of parrot in the world, including those recently extinct. Information is presented on the distribution, status, habitats and general habits. Almost 500 species and subspecies are illustrated in full color on large color plates.

Hard cover, 584 pages, 9½ x 12½"

Almost 300 large color plates depicting close to 500 different parrots; many line illustrations

PARROTS AND RELATED BIRDS
By Henry J. Bates and Robert L. Busenbark
ISBN 0-87666-967-4 New Edition
TFH H-912

This is the "bible" for parrot lovers. It has more color photographs and more information on parrots than any other single book on the subject. One of the bestselling books on our list. New editions are issued regularly, with new color photographs added with each new edition. Written primarily for the owner of more than one parrot or parrot-like bird. A necessary reference work for libraries, pet shops, and airport officials who must identify imported birds.

TAMING AND TRAINING PARROTS
By Dr. E. Mulawka
ISBN 0-87666-989-5
TFH H-109

This book deals effectively with Dr. Mulawka's proven methods of successful parrot training. In this volume, which is heavily illustrated with both color and black and white photographs, the author imparts his techniques for cultivating your pet parrot's innate abilities to learn.

Hard cover, 5½ x8", 349 pp.

152 full-color photos, 26 black and white photos

TRAINING YOUR PARROT
By Kevin P. Murphy
ISBN 0-87666-872-4
TFH H-1056

For anyone interested in making sure that he gets the most from a parrot or parrots by way of the satisfaction of owning a bird that will be a true companion instead of just an avian boarder. Loaded with good advice and full-color photos. Ages 13 and up.
Hard cover, 5½ x 8", 192 pages Illustrated with full-color and black and white photos.

This book is available in a new edition; more color photos are now included in the book in addition to updated nomenclature, and the structure of the book has been revised for easier reading.
Hard cover, 5½ x 8", 494 pages 107 black and white photos, 160 color photos

THE GREY PARROT
By Wolfgang de Grahl
ISBN 0-86622-495-5
T.F.H. H-1088

Well known as an authority and writer on parrots, author Wolfgang deGrahl proceeds to discuss matters of selection, housing, feeding, and care. The information and expertise offered here, illustrated with 80 black and white and color photographs and presented in an enjoyable way, make THE GREY PARROT an outstanding addition to the literature on parrots.
Hardcover, 6 x 9", 224 pages 80 full-color and black and white photos

Index